THE GEOGRAPHY DETECTIVE

INVESTIGATES

Farming

Jen Green

WAYLAND

First published in 2011 by Wayland

Copyright © Wayland 2011

Wayland
338 Euston Road
London NW1 3BH

Wayland Australia
Level 17/207 Kent Street
Sydney, NSW 2000

Senior editor: Debbie Foy
Designer: Stephen Prosser
Consultant: Nick Rowles
Picture researcher: Shelley Noronha
Artwork: Catherine Ward
Proofreader & indexer: Sarah Doughty

British Library Cataloguing in Publication Data

Green, Jen.
    Maps and map skills. -- (The geography
    detective investigates)
    1. Maps--Juvenile literature.
    2. Map reading--Juvenile literature.
    I. Title II. Series
    912-dc22

ISBN: 978 0 7502 6262 0

Printed in China

Wayland is a division of Hachette Children's Books,
an Hachette UK company

www.hachette.co.uk

Picture Acknowledgements:
Cover image: Bill Sykes/Cultura/Corbis
P1 Chris Knapton/Science Photo Library (repeat
p26): P4 © Frank and Helena/cultura/Corbis; P5
Istock; P7 Chris Close/Getty Images; P9b 047713
Erik Schaffer/Ecoscene; P10 DEA/G.Dagli
Orti/Getty Images; P11 David Wootton/Ecoscene;
P12 Nick Hawkes/Ecoscene; P13 Istock; P15
Graeme Norways/Getty Images; P16 GaryJohn
Norman/Getty Images; P17 Dorling
Kindersley/Getty Images; P18 AFP/Getty Images;
P19 Istock; P21 AFP/Getty Images; P22b David
Paterson/Getty Images; P22tr Shutterstock; P23
David Noton/Getty Images; P25 Anne
Rippy/Getty Images; P26 Chris Knapton/Science
Photo Library; P27 Inga Spence/ Getty Images;
P29 Istock. All other illustrations © Wayland.

Contents

Words that appear in **bold** can be found in the glossary on page 30.

🐾 **The Geography Detective, Sherlock Bones, will help you learn all about farming. The answers to Sherlock's questions can be found on page 31.**

What is farming?

Farming is the world's single most important occupation. It provides our food, wool and cotton for clothing, medicines and other products. Farming began around 10,000 years ago as people began to plant crops and rear livestock in the Middle East, and later India and China. As the first fields were ploughed, people began to settle in one place instead of wandering in search of wild plant and animal foods. Villages and towns grew up. Gradually, increased food production allowed some people to take up other trades, and so civilisation developed.

For centuries, farming was the main way of life in Britain and all over the world. However, most farmers were only able to grow enough food to feed their own families. This is called **subsistence farming**. From the 1700s, European farmers invented more scientific methods and machines to do work such as sowing and harvesting. The machines saved huge amounts of effort, but meant that fewer farm workers were needed. People began moving from the countryside to cities to earn a living.

FOCUS ON

Cereal crops

Just three crops: wheat, maize and rice provide over half the world's food. These are grain crops, also known as **cereals**. Like all crops, cereals require particular growing conditions. For example, rice needs a lot of moisture, so it is grown in flooded fields called **paddies**.

A patchwork of farmland in rural England.

In the last century, the world's human population grew very quickly. Farming has needed to become increasingly efficient to provide enough food for everyone. Most farms in the UK are now run on a commercial scale, and land that once provided food for just one family now feeds 100 people. As farms have modernised, so fewer people are involved in agriculture. Modern farming methods are not always good for the environment. This book will explore how farming developed, how modern farms are run and how they affect the natural world.

City farms often grow up on waste ground such as old factory land. They often mainly rear livestock but sometimes crops are also grown.

DETECTIVE WORK

Find out about the types of farming in your area. Do local farmers mainly grow crops or rear livestock? What are the chief crops or animals? City farms are found in or near large towns and cities. Find out about city farms using the Internet or local library.

What do crops need to grow?

Crops and all plants need sunlight, moisture and minerals from the soil to grow and flourish. Given these conditions, plants are able to manufacture their own food through **photosynthesis**. The green parts of a plant such as leaves use sunlight energy to convert carbon dioxide from the air, and water and minerals from the soil into sugars and starches for growth. In so doing they provide food for people and animals.

All crops require moisture. Most parts of the UK have plentiful rainfall which allows crops to flourish. However, in drier parts of the world crops have to be **irrigated** using water channelled from rivers, lakes or wells. Crops such as soya beans, and especially rice, need huge amounts of water. As the chart shows, livestock such as beef cattle are fed grain that needs a lot of water to grow. Seventy per cent of all fresh water available to us is used in agriculture.

FOCUS ON

Teeming with life

Huge numbers of earthworms, insects and micro-organisms live in the soil. They help to keep soil fertile by breaking down plant and animal remains. Earthworm burrows allow air and water down into the soil.

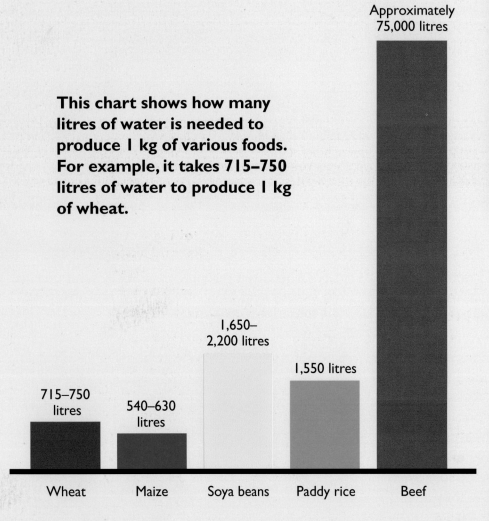

This chart shows how many litres of water is needed to produce 1 kg of various foods. For example, it takes 715–750 litres of water to produce 1 kg of wheat.

Approximately 75,000 litres

1,650–2,200 litres

1,550 litres

715–750 litres

540–630 litres

Wheat   Maize   Soya beans   Paddy rice   Beef

🐾 **Look at the chart. Which crop requires more water, soya beans or wheat?**

Soil is a vital resource for farmers. It enables crops to grow and provides essential **nutrients**. The top layer of soil is a mixture of rocky fragments and plant and animals remains, known as **humus**. Soil takes a long time to form, as wind, frost and water break rocks into pieces. Plants take root among the rocky fragments, and later rot to enrich the soil. Growing the same crop year after year can exhaust soil by removing particular minerals from the soil, which are used up by the crops. Farmers can restore nutrients using artificial fertilisers or by ploughing in the remains of crops.

Ploughing turns the soil, allowing air and water to penetrate. This is called aeration. The topsoil is rich in humus.

DETECTIVE WORK

Investigate the tiny animals that live in soil by putting a small amount of soil in a sieve. Balance the sieve on a large empty jar and place under a lamp. After an hour or so, as the soil heats up, tiny creatures drop into the jar. Tip them onto a piece of paper and examine them with a magnifying glass. Put them back outside when you have finished. Always wash your hands after handling soil.

What are the main types of farming?

The type of farming that goes on in a particular region depends partly on natural conditions such as climate, the height of the land and the soil. In the UK, crops are traditionally grown in the fertile soil of sheltered plains and valleys, while livestock are grazed on higher ground. However, modern methods allow farmers to improve natural conditions and so grow a greater variety of crops.

The two main types of farming are **arable farming** and livestock farming. Most farms specialise in growing just one or two crops or rearing a particular type of animal. Growing the same crop year after year is called **monoculture**. Mixed farms have crops and livestock.

Wheat, oats and barley are the main cereals grown in the UK. Root vegetables such as **sugar beet** and potatoes are also popular. Each crop requires a particular time to ripen – this is called the growing season. This means that various crops suit different locations. Northern Britain has a cool climate with a five-month growing season, which is suitable for oats and barley. Southern Britain has a warmer climate with an eight-month growing season, which suits a wider range of cereals and vegetables.

The map above shows average temperatures and rainfall in the British Isles.

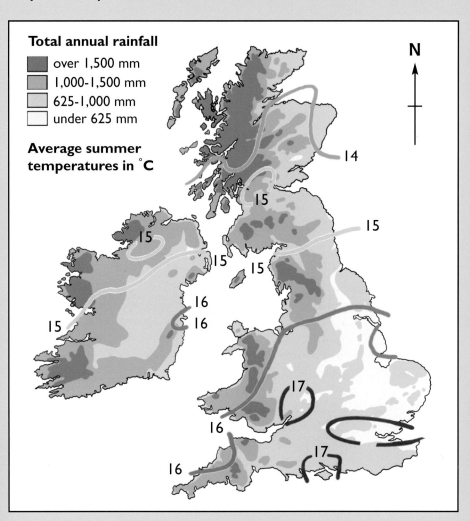

Total annual rainfall

- over 1,500 mm
- 1,000-1,500 mm
- 625-1,000 mm
- under 625 mm

Average summer temperatures in °C

N

14
15
15
15
15
15
15
16
16
15
17
16
17
16

DETECTIVE WORK

Use the Internet or a library to research the climate and soil where you live. Do you live in a hilly or lowland area? What is the average rainfall? How do local conditions suit the types of farming in your area?

This map shows the main types of farming in the UK. If you compare the two maps, you will start to see how climate affects farming.

Mountainous areas such as the Scottish Highlands and Snowdonia have a harsh climate, steep terrain and thin, stony soil. This land is unsuitable for arable farming, but sheep and beef cattle can be grazed. Dairy cattle (cows) thrive in lush lowland pastures of south-west England and south-west Scotland, which have high rainfall. Pigs and poultry do well on the flat, fertile lowlands of eastern England.

🐾 **Study the farming map. What is the main area for arable farming?**

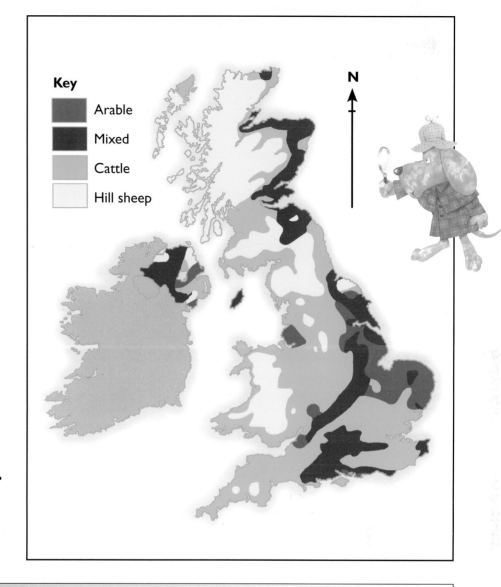

Key
- Arable
- Mixed
- Cattle
- Hill sheep

N

FOCUS ON

Market gardening

Fruits, vegetables and flowers are grown for sale on small-scale farms called **market gardens**. Crops such as tomatoes and peppers that require warm conditions may be reared in greenhouses. Growing under glass allows farmers to cultivate a wider range of crops. Most market gardens are located close to cities where the produce is transported and sold quickly, before it spoils.

Lettuce growing well in a market garden in Andalucia, Spain.

How did farming develop?

Farming is the world's oldest profession. It began as farmers started to cultivate crops for their edible seeds. Early farmers improved crop varieties by saving the best seeds for sowing. The first farm tools were made of wood and stone; later metal was invented. An early plough called the **ard** was invented around 6,000 BCE. By 3,000 BCE oxen were being used to pull ploughs.

All over the world, arable farming followed a regular cycle. The soil was prepared by ploughing and fertilising. Seeds were sown and weeds removed by hand. At harvest time, crops were reaped using **scythes**, then the grain was separated from the stalks (**threshing**) and from the husks (**winnowing**). For centuries this work remained largely unchanged, but in the 1700s farmers developed new farming methods and invented labour-saving machinery. This is called the Agricultural Revolution.

DETECTIVE WORK

Investigate the history of farming in your area. Local museums may have historic farm equipment, while public buildings may have old photos of farm workers. You can investigate at the library, or via the Internet – try typing 'history of farming' into a search engine.

This tomb painting from ancient Egypt shows a farmer reaping wheat with a sickle.

In 1701, British farmer Jethro Tull invented the **seed drill**. This horse-drawn drill cut parallel furrows in the soil and dropped seeds in the rows. In the mid-1700s efficient steam engines were developed. By the mid-1800s steam-powered tractors were being used to haul loads and drive ploughs and threshers. By the 1920s petrol-driven tractors were performing all kinds of work on farms in Europe and North America. Within 20 years they had replaced work animals such as shire horses. In the 1900s the arrival of electricity on farms paved the way for labour-saving devices, such as milking machines.

❧ **Put these inventions in the order they appeared: seed drill, electric milking machine, steam-driven tractor, ard.**

Combine harvesters are used to gather and process many different crops, including wheat, barley rice, soya beans and cotton.

FOCUS ON

Harvesting machines

The combine harvester is a complex machine which performs many different jobs during harvest. It cuts and gathers the crop, and then threshes and winnows the grain. Modern combine harvesters do the work of scores of farm labourers in a fraction of the time.

How has farming changed since 1950?

If you could travel back in time to a British farm before the Second World War, you would find that farming has been transformed in the last 70 to 80 years. Farms that once employed scores of labourers, and were largely powered by horses, are now run by just a few workers with the aid of machines.

From the early 1900s, farmers began to use artificial fertiliser on their fields. These chemicals provided all the nutrients needed for growth. This allowed farmers to grow the same crop year after year, which improved efficiency.

During the mid-1900s **pesticides** became available. These poisonous chemicals are used to kill crop pests such as weeds, insects and fungi. However, scientists later discovered that farm chemicals can harm the environment. Pesticides kill all kinds of wildlife, not just weeds and harmful insects. When fertilisers drain away into streams and rivers they cause tiny plants called **algae** to 'bloom' or multiply. This reduces oxygen levels in the water, which harms fish and other life.

DETECTIVE WORK

Look for signs of algae bloom on local streams and rivers. If waterways are covered with a green blanket of weeds, it is probably caused by fertilisers leaking from local farms.

When waterweed blankets the surface of a waterway, it makes the water low in oxygen, harming aquatic life.

During the 1940s scientists began to develop new varieties of wheat, rice and other crops which produced bumper harvests. Ten years later these **high-yield varieties**, or **HYV**s, were doubling or trebling harvests in Europe and North America. During the 1960s and 70s, 'supercrops' such as rice were introduced to other parts of the world, such as Africa and Asia. This development, called the **Green Revolution**, helped to reduce **famine** in poor countries, but also caused some problems. HYVs are only really effective when used alongside other technology, such as fertilisers, pesticides and modern machinery, which poor farmers in Africa and Asia could not afford. This forced some farmers out of business.

Tractors are used to spray pesticides in Britain. In the US small planes are used to treat large farms.

FOCUS ON

Killer chemical

In 1939, Swiss scientist Paul Muller developed a powerful new insecticide called DDT. By the 1950s, DDT was being used on farms all over the world. But in the 1960s scientists realised that it was killing all kinds of wildlife. Farmers in the West stopped using DDT, but it is still widely used in Africa and Asia.

What was the Green Revolution?

How are farms run as businesses?

As farming techniques have improved, so farms have become highly efficient. Modern farms are business enterprises, and farmers have to be skilled at finance as well as agriculture. Farming can be seen as a system based on the principle that farmers have to input certain things, in order to get a good **yield**, or output, and make a profit.

The diagram below shows the inputs and outputs involved in agriculture. Some of the inputs are provided by nature – sunlight, rain and soil encourage plant growth. The rest must be provided by the farmer. Arable farmers spend money on seeds, chemicals, labour and machinery. Livestock farmers invest in new animals, **fodder** and machinery. They must also pay for labour to maintain hedges, fences and walls, and check the stock.

FOCUS ON

Milk processing

The milk you pour on your breakfast cereal has passed through several processes. The cows are milked in a modern dairy. The milk is cooled and transported by tanker to a processing plant where it is sterilised using a heat-treatment called **pasteurisation**. It may then be packaged or bottled, or processed further to produce butter, cheese, yogurt or ice cream.

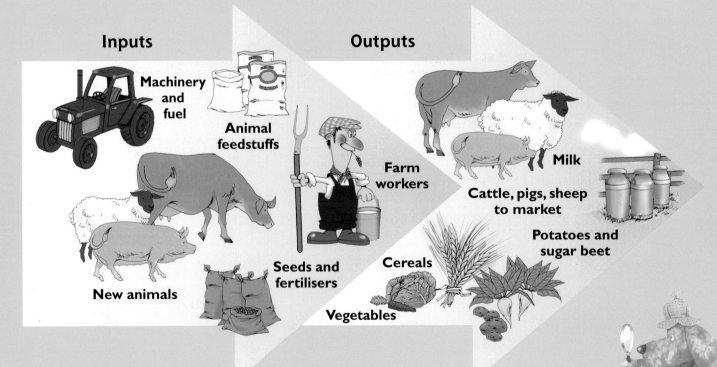

Inputs

Machinery and fuel

Animal feedstuffs

Farm workers

New animals

Seeds and fertilisers

Outputs

Milk

Cattle, pigs, sheep to market

Potatoes and sugar beet

Cereals

Vegetables

This diagram shows the inputs and outputs involved in arable and livestock farming.

Name three 'natural' inputs involved in arable and livestock farming.

The farmer must also decide whether to farm intensively or extensively. In **intensive farming**, the farmer invests heavily to get a high yield from every **hectare** of land. In **extensive farming**, the farmer who has a large amount of land to cultivate makes a lower outlay and so gains a lower yield from every hectare. The decision often depends on the money available to cover input costs.

The farmer's output of crops or livestock is really just the first stage in a long chain of production that puts food on the table. Almost all farm produce is processed before it reaches shops and supermarkets. For example, grain is ground into flour to make bread. Sunflower seeds are made into cooking oil. Pigs are slaughtered and processed to make pork and bacon. Food processing is a major industry which provides many jobs, but also makes food more expensive.

Dairy cows are normally milked twice a day. Modern milking machines collect milk from many animals as once.

DETECTIVE WORK

Make a list of all the foods you have eaten today in one column on a piece of paper. List the farm produce used to make the foods in a second column. Some foods contain many products. If you are not sure of the ingredients, check the packaging.

How do modern livestock farms work?

Livestock farming began at least 9,000 years ago. In the UK, the most important farm animals are beef and dairy cattle, sheep, pigs and chickens, which are reared for meat, milk, wool and eggs. Farmers look after their animals by providing the basics: food, water and shelter. Some crops are grown specifically for animal fodder. The animals' health is checked regularly and medicines given where needed.

Many livestock farmers in the UK now use intensive methods, sometimes called 'factory farming'. The animals are kept indoors in controlled conditions, and fed an exact mix of nutrients, including grain and fishmeal. On some farms the feed also contains medicines called **antibiotics** and chemical hormones to speed up growth. Pigs are reared in sheds called fattening houses, while hens are kept in cages on battery farms. Some people think that keeping animals in cramped conditions is cruel. The livestock farmers argue that intensive farming is more efficient and helps to keep prices low, which suits shoppers.

Hens on a battery farm are kept in stacked wire cages. Food and water are dispensed automatically. The eggs roll on to a conveyer belt.

DETECTIVE WORK

Ask your teacher if you can have a class debate on factory farming. Discuss the advantages and disadvantages of the intensive and free-range systems. Make a list of pupils who are for and against the 'factory farming' method.

Free-range pigs being reared outdoors on a UK farm.

Free-range livestock farming is an alternative method of farming animals in factory conditions. Animals such as pigs and chickens are allowed to roam more freely outdoors. Free-range products have been popular since the 1990s. Meat and eggs produced in this way are a bit more expensive, but many shoppers are willing to pay more for food that they believe tastes better and is more healthy. Critics of the free-range method say it uses up more land, which can put wild habitats at risk.

Stock breeding methods

For centuries farmers improved their stock by breeding from their best animals. In this way many distinct breeds developed. Crossbreeds combine the best characteristics of two breeds. For example, a hardy sheep may be crossed with a top wool-producer to produce a hardy wool-producer. Many modern breeders use a technique called artificial insemination. Sperm taken from the male is used to fertilise the female. In this way a prize bull can fertilise many cows.

Where does our food come from?

In the UK most of our food comes from supermarkets. The big supermarket chains offer a huge range of products, with tens of thousands of different items. The foods are sourced from all over the world. Fifty years ago shoppers had much less choice. People brought fruits and vegetables produced locally when they were in season. Now we can buy exotic fruits and vegetables, such as strawberries, mangoes, pineapples and artichokes at any time of year.

Bananas are unloaded from a truck ready to be packed and transported from the tropics to countries such as the UK. Bananas are picked green and ripen during transportation.

FOCUS ON

Fairtrade

Fairtrade is a trading movement that aims to give growers in tropical countries a fair price for their crops. Fairtrade goods such as tea, coffee, chocolate and bananas are more expensive, but the extra provides growers with a fair deal and a better wage. Look out for Fairtrade products in shops and supermarkets.

Much of the produce on supermarket shelves comes from tropical regions such as Africa, Asia and the Caribbean. Foods such as tea, coffee, sugar and bananas are grown on large plantations. The governments of tropical countries encourage farmers to grow crops for export, known as **cash crops**, because it brings in foreign money that the country can use to develop its economy. However, the supermarket chains that buy the produce are very powerful. They often offer low prices, which means that farm workers in the tropics earn a very low wage.

Many of the goods sold at supermarkets have travelled thousands of kilometres by plane, ship, train and truck. Transporting foods across the world uses huge amounts of fuel and is very expensive. Burning all that fuel also causes a lot of air pollution. You can help to reduce 'food miles' – the distance travelled by foods – by encouraging your family to buy goods that are produced close to home, and fruit and vegetables in season.

We eat more meat nowadays than people did 30 years ago. Some meats, such as New Zealand lamb, travel halfway round the world to reach our tables.

DETECTIVE WORK
Most foods are labelled with information about the country of origin (where the food is grown). Next time your family does a food shop, check the labels. You could copy or trace a world map and mark all the countries of origin. Which food product has travelled the furthest?

🐾 Much of the lamb sold in UK supermarkets comes from New Zealand. Find New Zealand on a world map. Study the map's scale. Can you estimate roughly how far the meat has travelled to reach the UK?

Can farmers grow enough food for everyone?

Food production has increased rapidly in the last 30 years, but the population has risen even faster. By around 2012 there will be 7 billion people on Earth, and by 2040 there may be 9 billion. How can farmers keep pace with the demand for food?

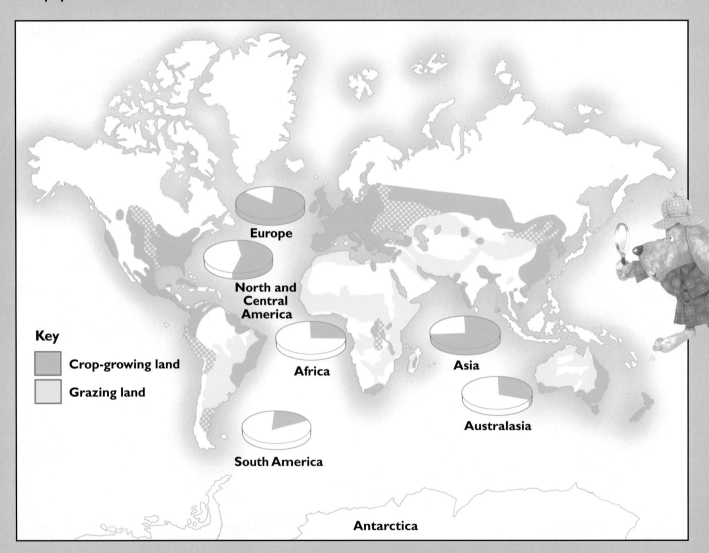

Key

Crop-growing land

Grazing land

Europe

North and Central America

Africa

Asia

Australasia

South America

Antarctica

Only about half of the world's land area can be cultivated or used for pasture. The rest is too dry, wet, steep or stony.

Across the world, around 800 million people don't get enough to eat. In Africa one in every five people goes hungry. Meanwhile in the West, huge amounts of food are wasted, and many people overeat. Being overweight is a growing problem, including among young people. How has this situation come about?

🐾 **Study the map. Which continents have relatively little land under cultivation?**

The world's farmers currently grow enough food to feed everyone on Earth, but unfortunately, that food is unevenly distributed. Regions where the population is rising fast, such as Africa, Asia and South America, are often places where farming is difficult, because of poor soil and unreliable weather. When extreme weather such as droughts, floods or hurricanes strike, crops are ruined and famine results.

Charities provide funding to help farmers work more efficiently, or restart their lives after a disaster such as drought.

FOCUS ON

Tackling famine

What is being done to tackle food shortages? Groups such as the United Nations' Food and Agriculture Organisation (FAO) are working to improve farming methods and co-ordinate food production. They provide funding for inputs such as machinery, fertiliser, irrigation projects or livestock. In 2000, the UN set the goal of halving the number of people who suffer from hunger by 2015.

In contrast, modern farming techniques in wealthy nations such as the UK mean that farmers are able to grow more food than is needed. The **surplus** may be sold for **export**, but all too often it goes to waste. In Europe, surplus milk has been poured down old mine shafts. Sometimes surplus food can be used to feed people in famine-struck regions, but often, the costs of transporting the food before it spoils are too high.

DETECTIVE WORK

Find out more about the work of the FAO by logging onto www.fao.org. Charities such as Oxfam work to relieve famine. Find out more about this on www.oxfam.org.uk. You could organise a sponsored walk, cycle or swim to raise money for famine relief.

How does farming affect the environment?

Farming changes the landscape and can cause problems for nature. When wild land is converted to farmland, it causes **habitat loss**. Farm chemicals can poison wildlife. Farming can cause erosion and **deplete** water sources. However, sensitively managed farmland can support a range of wildlife.

Centuries ago, Britain and most of Europe were covered in woodland, which was cut down to create farmland. Wild meadows were ploughed up, and wetlands drained. Native plants and animals lost their habitats. Britain became a mosaic of small fields, which were at least surrounded by hedges which sheltered mammals, birds and insects. However in the 1960s and 70s, many of these hedges were dug up to make larger fields where tractors and combine harvesters could operate. This created difficulties for wildlife. The use of pesticides further reduced **biodiversity** – the variety of species in an area.

The corncrake (above), a bird once common on UK farms, all but died out following the arrival of combine harvesters, which disturbed its breeding habits.

The removal of hedges and use of pesticides reduces biodiversity in the countryside.

Wildlife such as birds and hedgehogs thrive in hedges and wild borders left on the edge of fields, called 'set-aside' land.

The roots of wild trees, hedges and grasses help to bind the soil together. When natural vegetation is removed, it makes the land vulnerable to **erosion**. Heavy rain can wash the soil away, while dry weather can turn it to dust, so it blows away on the wind. Where farmers allow livestock to overgraze pastures, the ground can also be stripped bare.

DETECTIVE WORK

Britain's hedges are made of woody shrubs such as blackthorn, hawthorn, hazel, dogrose, honeysuckle and bramble. Experts say it takes 100 years for each species to get established. So hedges can be roughly dated by counting the number of species. See how many species you can find in a farmland hedge.

🐾 **Estimate the age of a hedge that contains hawthorn, hazel, dogrose and honeysuckle.**

In dry places such as Africa and Australia, farming is putting pressure on water sources such as rivers, lakes and wells. So much water is being drawn off that some rivers are running dry. Sprinkler systems used in irrigation use huge amounts of water. Too-frequent irrigation can also cause natural salts in the ground to rise to the surface, making the soil too salty for farming. This problem is known as salinisation.

FOCUS ON

Helping nature

As a member of the European Union (EU), British farmers follow a set of rules called the Common Agricultural Policy (CAP for short). In the 1960s and 70s, CAP was all about increasing productivity on farms and producing cheap food, but now measures such as the Environmental Stewardship Scheme aim to protect nature. Under this scheme EU farmers can get grants for restoring wetlands or replanting hedges and woodlands.

What is organic farming?

Modern industrial-style farming causes problems for the environment. **Organic farming** is an alternative method of farming that is more in tune with nature. It is also more sustainable – this means that farmers are able to produce food without harming the soil or causing pollution, which would make it more difficult to farm in future.

Organic farming is a way of farming without using chemicals. Instead of artificial fertilisers, organic farmers use manure, plant waste or seaweed to add nutrients to the soil. Instead of using pesticides to kill crop-eating insects such as aphids, they encourage natural predators such as ladybirds. Growing a variety of different crops instead of just one, year after year, helps to prevent the build-up of pests and disease. So does a practice called **intercropping**. This means growing alternate rows of different crops, such as onions and potatoes.

Crop rotation

Crop rotation is the practice of varying the crops that are grown in fields, often in a four-year cycle. For example, the farmer may rotate barley, turnips, wheat and peas. Crops called **legumes,** such as peas or beans, help restore nitrogen, one of the essential nutrients, to the soil. Crop rotation was used by Roman farmers. It partly fell out of use in the second half of the twentieth century, but is becoming popular again.

This diagram shows a four-year crop rotation.

Organic farmers use a mixture of modern techniques and traditional methods, such as crop rotation.

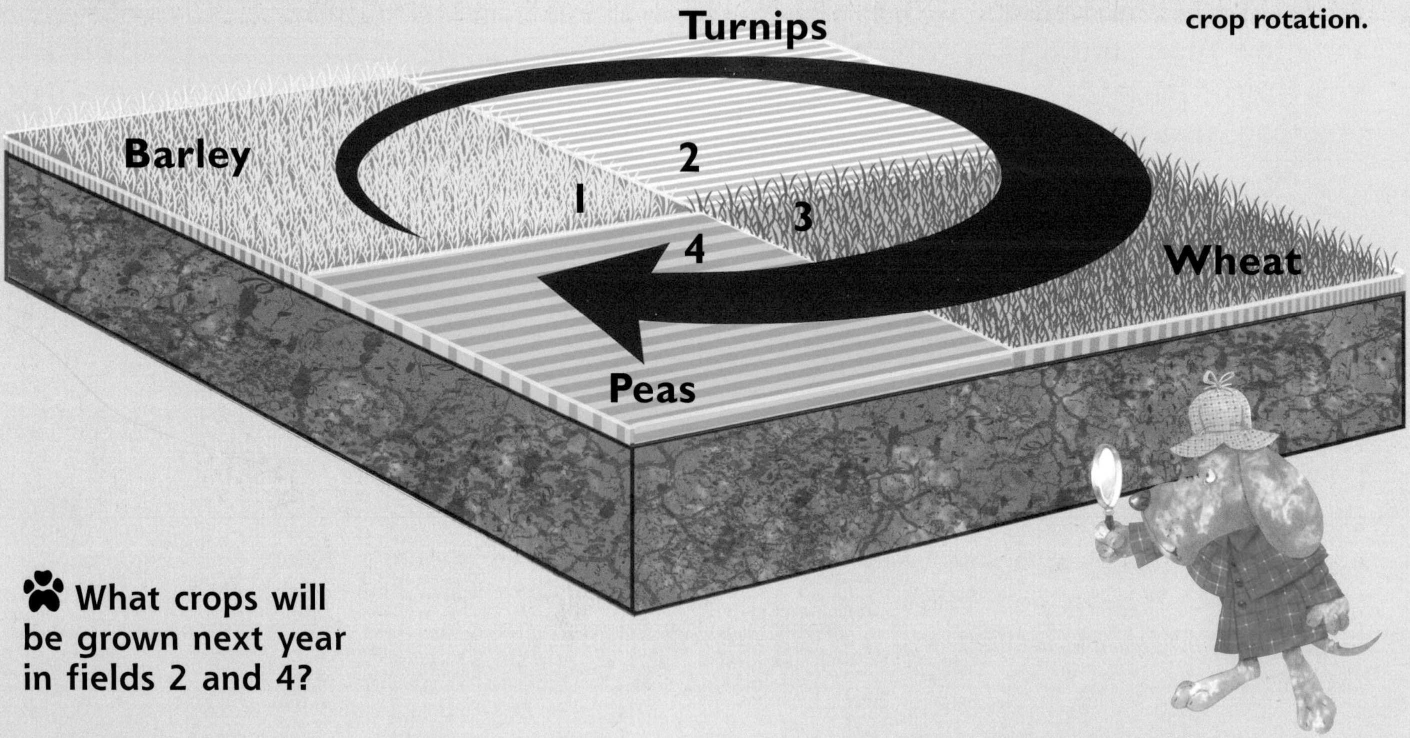

Turnips

Barley

2

1

3

4

Wheat

Peas

What crops will be grown next year in fields 2 and 4?

Organic livestock farmers use free-range methods. They don't put antibiotics and growth hormones in animal feed. As far as possible, the animals are fed with fodder grown locally. This helps to cut down 'food miles' – as does the practice of selling food at local shops and markets. Despite being more expensive than other produce, sales of organic foods such as milk, meat, fruit and vegetables soared in the 1990s. One disadvantage is that both arable and livestock organic farming take up more land. This can put pressure on wild habitats.

Organic fruit and vegetables may be less 'perfect' than produce grown using chemicals, but many people feel they taste better.

DETECTIVE WORK

Look for organic produce such as fruit and vegetables in shops and supermarkets. Compare prices with other produce that is grown intensively. Do organic fruit and vegetables look different to varieties produced using chemicals? Why do you think this is?

What is the future of farming?

Farming has been transformed in the last 50 years. New technology and scientific breakthroughs have made farming more productive. In the twenty-first century, farmers will need to find new, ever-more efficient methods in order to satisfy the growing need for food.

Farmers have always improved crops and livestock by selective breeding. In the past, this process happened slowly, over many generations. Now scientists are able to directly alter the genetic makeup of living organisms through **genetic engineering**. Genes from other plants can be added to crops to produce varieties that are bigger or more able to resist pests, drought or frost. The new varieties are called **genetically modified organisms (GMOs)**. Some people believe that GMOs will help to tackle world hunger. Others feel that this technology needs further testing before we can be sure it is safe. In the UK and most of Europe, GMOs are grown in laboratory conditions, but they are now widely grown in North America.

Some believe that GMOs should not be grown on open farmland as they might cross-breed with other crops. This could result in 'superweeds', that are frost or drought resistant.

DETECTIVE WORK

Ask your family and friends what they think about GM crops. Should Britain take the lead in developing this new technology, or is further testing needed? List your results in two columns, for and against.

Earth's climate is changing. In the 1990s, scientists discovered that world temperatures were rising. This is called **global warming**. Scientists now believe that global warming is caused by increased levels of so-called **greenhouse gases**, which are given off when fuels are burned. Farm animals such as cattle also produce greenhouse gas. Scientists believe that global warming may well make the weather more extreme in future. Droughts, floods and storms could all become more common.

Climate change is likely to affect farming patterns, presenting new challenges for the world's farmers. Wet areas could experience more floods. Meanwhile dry areas could suffer more drought. In the twenty-first century, people may need to farm new areas to produce enough food. This will put growing pressure on wild habitats. It will also stretch water sources, so irrigation needs to become more efficient.

FOCUS ON

Conserving water

Drip feeding is a modern technique which uses little water. A network of pipes drip moisture on to plant roots. Drip feeding uses far less water than sprinkler systems, so it could help to conserve the world's precious water supplies.

A corn field in the USA that has been damaged by drought and hail.

Your project

If you've been doing the detective work throughout the book and answered all of Sherlock's questions, you now know a lot about arable and livestock farming! You could use this knowledge to produce your own project about farming.

Practical project

• The best way to find out about farming is to grow your own vegetables or flowers. Ask your headteacher if you can have a small patch of garden or a corner of the school grounds to cultivate tomatoes and lettuces. If no outdoor space is available, you could grow mustard and cress in a tray lined with damp tissue paper or cotton wool.

• Prepare the soil and sow the seeds. When the plants come up, water them regularly. Don't use weedkiller or slug pellets if you want to farm organically. Harvest the crop when it is ready and prepare a tasty sandwich with what you have grown. Home-grown lettuce, cress and tomatoes taste delicious!

Topics to investigate

• Find out about how farming methods and the way of life have changed on a local farm over the years. You could ask to interview a farmer or use local libraries or the Internet for your research.

• Compare farming methods on two farms in different parts of the world. If possible, one should be in a tropical country. Are the farms large or small? What crops are grown or animals reared? How is farming adapted to local conditions? What happens to the produce?

• Find out more about food shortages and famine. Where are the places where people are hungry? Mark the locations on a world map. Are food shortages caused by natural disasters such as floods or drought, or are there other causes, such as war or overgrazing?

• Find out about all the work that goes on a local farm. How many people are employed on the farm? How does the work on the farm change through the year?

Your local library and the Internet can provide all sorts of information. Try the websites listed on page 31. You might like to present the information in an interesting way, using the ideas on the opposite page.

Project presentation

- Imagine you are making a TV documentary or writing a magazine article about farming. Make a plan to organise your material. Start with an introduction and draw conclusions at the end.

- Write a story or poem from the point of view of a farmer, farm worker or an animal, such as a free-range pig, dairy cow or battery chicken. Describe how life on the farm changes through the year.

🐾 Sherlock has done a project about a working farm dog, the border collie. These helpful dogs herd the sheep and guard the farm!

A border collie helps a farmer round up the flock on a farm in the English countryside.

Glossary

Algae Tiny plants that grow in water or damp places.

Antibiotic A drug used to cure illness in people and animals.

Arable farming Growing crops.

Ard A primitive plough.

Biodiversity The variety of life in a particular habitat.

Cash crop A crop that is grown for export (sale abroad).

Cereals A grain crop such as wheat, rice, oats and barley.

Crop rotation The practice of changing the crops that are grown in fields from year to year.

Deplete To use up or exhaust a resource.

Erosion When rock or soil is worn away by wind, running water or ice.

Export To sell a product abroad.

Extensive farming A method of farming which involves a low input from the farmer to gain a relatively low yield per hectare of land.

Famine An extreme shortage of food.

Fodder A word used to describe animal feed.

Genetic engineering The process by which scientists alter the characteristics of living things by adding genes from different species.

Genetically modified organism (GMO) A species or variety created by genetic engineering.

Global warming Rising temperatures worldwide, caused by an increase of gases in the atmosphere that trap the Sun's heat.

Greenhouse gas One of a group of gases that contribute to global warming.

Green Revolution The research and spread of modern intensive agriculture, which increased world harvests in the mid-1900s.

Habitat loss When a wild habitat is destroyed or changed by people.

Hectare A metric unit of area equal to 100 acres (or 10,000 square metres).

High-yield variety (HYV) A food crop developed to produce a large harvest.

Humus A rich layer of rotting plant and animal matter in the soil.

Intensive farming A type of agriculture in which farmers use chemicals and modern machinery and methods to produce a high yield per hectare.

Intercropping The practice of growing several crops together in a field.

Irrigate To water the land using water drawn from rivers, lakes or wells.

Legume A plant belonging to the pea and bean family.

Market garden A small-scale farm where vegetables, flowers and fruit are grown for sale at nearby villages and towns.

Monoculture Growing the same crop year after year.

Nutrients Nourishing chemicals which plants need to grow.

Organic farming A method of farming without using chemical fertilisers and pesticides.

Paddies Flooded fields used to grow rice.

Pasteurisation The process of heating milk, or another liquid, briefly in order to kill germs.

Pesticide A chemical used to kill weeds, insects or fungi that harm crops.

Photosynthesis The process by which plants manufacture their own food using sunlight energy.

Scythe A curved tool used to reap (cut) crops.

Seed drill A machine used for sowing seeds.

Subsistence farming When farmers are only able to grow enough food to feed their families, with little left over to sell.

Sugar beet A root vegetable.

Surplus An amount left over that is often not needed.

Threshing Separating grain from the stalks.

Winnowing Separating grain from the husks.

Yield The amount of harvest from a crop.

Answers

☙ **Page 6:** It takes more water to produce 1 kg of soya beans than 1 kg of wheat.

☙ **Page 9:** East Anglia in eastern Britain is the main area for arable farming, with smaller pockets of arable land elsewhere.

☙ **Page 11:** Ard, seed drill, steam-driven tractor, electric milking machine.

☙ **Page 13:** The Green Revolution was the name given to the development and spread of new, industrial-style agriculture and high-yielding crops throughout the world.

☙ **Page 14:** Natural inputs involved in arable and livestock farming include sunshine, rain and soil which help create pasture.

☙ **Page 19:** The direct distance between Auckland, New Zealand and London, UK is 18,300 kilometres.

☙ **Page 20:** A relatively small percentage of Africa, Australasia and South America is used for arable farming. Antarctica is uncultivated.

☙ **Page 23:** The presence of the four woody shrubs suggests that a hedge could be up to 400 years old.

☙ **Page 24:** Barley will be grown next year in field 2, with wheat in field 4.

Further information

Further reading

Food and Farming, series by Richard and Louise Spilsbury; Ian Graham (Wayland 2009)

Food and the World, Julia Allen and Margaret Iggulden, (Franklin Watts, 2005)

Food and Farming, Pam Robson, (Franklin Watts, 2001)

Websites

Defra: UK government site for the environment, food and rural affairs: ww2.defra.gov.uk/environment

The Food and Farming website provides information about food, famine and organic farming: www.foodandfarming.org

The Soil Association, UK has information about organic farming: www.soilassociation.org.uk

Fair Trade Movement information:
Fairtrade foundation: www.fairtrade.org.uk
Make trade fair: www.maketradefair.com

Aid agencies concerned with providing help on farming, famine and water conservation. Their websites are as follows:

Food and Agriculture Organisation of the United Nations (FAO): www.fao.org

Water Aid: www.wateraid.org.uk

Oxfam: www.oxfam.org.uk

Farm Africa: www.farmafrica.org.uk

Index

The Geography Detective Investigates

Contents of titles in the series:

WAYLAND